CLOUDBREAK

HEATHER SAUNDERS ESTES

Cover & interior photograph by Fraser Cottrell
Author photograpy by Nate Reyes

Copyright © 2021 HEATHER SAUNDERS ESTES
ISBN: 978-1-63649-690-0

Poetic Matrix Press
www.poeticmatrix.com

ACKNOWLEDGMENTS

Heather would like to acknowledge the editors of the following publications in which some of the poems in *Cloudbreak* appeared or are about to be published: *Fog and Light—San Francisco through the Eyes of the Poets Who Live Here* edited by Diane Frank; *Swimming in Deep Blue; The Sky Away from Here; Bach In the Afternoon; Pandemic Puzzle Poems—An Anthology;* as well as the journals *Sisyphus, Vistas & Byways, and Brine.*

Thank you to my wonderful husband Fred, daughter Laurel and our shelter-in-place family friend Valerie Laura Jade.My patient friends, Kathy and Cindy and my writing group are sources of joy, support and community. Much appreciation to Diane Frank, Kwame Dawes, Barry Goldensohn, and other inspirational poets and writers whose expertise continues to improve my craft of writing.

Sincere acknowledgment to my colleagues at Planned Parenthood Northern California and the individual clients whom I have had the honor and pleasure to work with and serve for so many years.

CONTENTS

CLOUDBREAK

I DUST OFF MY HANDS

BIG THIS WAY

PULL OF THE EDGE

THERE IS A MOMENT

ABOUT THE AUTHOR

FOR MOM AND DAD

Thank you for sharing your love
of words, curiosity, rebellion, and justice.

Cloudbreak

I Dust Off My Hands

BENEDICTION

Today the sky is threaded
in folds of gray raw silk.
Luminous catches of sun
gleam in its cloth.
Not light and gauzy,
or stretched smooth and matte,
although I have seen such fabric skies.

One winter morning, my father
and I drove to school together.
Peering through the car's front windshield
at the growing storm clouds he said—
You know what I will miss the most when I die?
He was not thinking about the impact
of that vision on a doting 12-year-old daughter.
Not seeing the sky and clouds, he whispered.

Or maybe he said that when I was in second grade,
our necks craned back
to scan a mackerel-scaled sky,
cirrus streams of mares' tails
caught in frozen winds of the troposphere.

THE BIG DIG

I was 5 years old when it began—
the hole in our backyard.
The goal, to dig to the other side of the world,
was my father's inspired "painting the fence" project
for my mutinous, restless brother.
The shoveled dirt would do double duty
in our garden compost pile.

I was warned. Don't fall in.
There were shouts and screeching metallic scrapes
when a spade hit something large.
I was breathless for a treasure chest.
Glacial rocks were levered out with grunts, manly huzzahs.
Bits of archaeological broken crockery emerged.
My job was to use the hose to wash and imagine
who had used this piece of blue-figured plate.
More often, they unearthed pupating grubs
and roots of nearby mulberry trees.

Over the years, the hole was abandoned, ignored,
clogged with rain and leaves.
I secretly visited by myself. Dug alone.
Never got to China or even bedrock
but I found proud blisters on my hands,
sore muscles, and frontier
under my fingernails.

THE FIRST DAY OF SUMMER

I lie naked on my bed
in the middle of the week.
Big windows open to the sky.
Sunlight friendly and
cat-warm on the golden oak boards.
A slight breeze stirs my skin.
My hands slide across my body,
soft, even softer as I get older.
My breasts were full of milk,
twenty-four years ago.
Now resting under my fingers
is the smooth neat scar of the C-section.
Hip replacement traces
are on each thigh.
I sigh with satisfaction
for a job well done.
She, my body and I,
have been together for years.
Skin all new
many times over
since I sat on a different bed,
seventeen years young.
Wet from the shower,
I brushed my long brown hair
promising myself that years later
I would remember this moment.
By then, I imagined,
my body would also be
loved by another.
I did, and I am.

MEMORY

Monet stood shivering in the cold.
Before him, a snow-filled pasture
and lavender reflecting on the wings
of a solitary black and white bird.

I remember a moment with my father.
He had entrusted the full length of a milled two by four
balanced upright on its end, to me.
He placed my child hands around it to hold
while he selected a tool for our porch repair.

I remember the pride I felt.
I remember the smell of the wood beam, cool against my cheek.
I remember how straight and tall it was as I looked up to the sky
to squint at its wobbling top end.

My hands lost control and it toppled over
quickly and decisively
with a deafening, cataclysmic crash,
smashing into the windshield of our family car.
I remember a moment of real fear.

I don't remember if I was crying, but I expect so.
I remember surprise, disbelief and relief
when my father crouched down to me,
he could see that I couldn't control it.
"It wasn't your fault. It's OK."

I wonder if it happened that way?
My memory is a storyteller.
Maybe I need time and distance to remember.
Perhaps memory doesn't matter to truth.

Monet could have taken a photograph.
It would have been without wind, or
the sweep of the magpie's blue-black wings—
without the scent of my Dad bending down
to put his arm around me and wipe my tears.

Into My Hidden Forest

Cadmium-yellow forsythia bushes
interlock their twiggy arms creating private spaces.
Slender stems sweep the ground.
I push aside flowers, crawl under on hands and knees,
reclose the cascade curtain.

The hollow becomes a hidden castle,
shell cottage on a sea cliff,
Count of Monte Cristo cell, *Secret Garden*,
bower library with *The Sword in the Stone*.

I hang trinkets above my head—
branches like stalactites
or glittering Christmas ornaments.
A mended porcelain teacup holds apple juice,
honeyed mead, sacred spring water.

I brush away pebbles and sticks
to gouge a dirt hollow for a garden nest.
There I recline on a castoff woolen blanket
with blue satin binding. Leaves crinkle.
Damp earth is in my nose and on the tips of my fingers.

Bees nuzzle into yellow flowers.
Fuzzy undersides exposed
as they buzz away.
Beetles tap-dance along curved buttresses.
Far away, a mockingbird sings in robin and crow.

A sparrow comes looking for seeds.
Surprised to find me, it stops, tilts its head,
a question in black eyes.
Finding the answer, it continues to hop
and scratch with sharp claws in the leaf litter.

So it made perfect sense when the woodchuck
stuck her black nose
through my branch curtains
and asked—
Where is the hole to the other side of the earth?

LAND PARK FALL

Leaf blowers are harsh in crisp morning air.
I prefer rhythmic raking with bamboo
in the timeless connection to peasants
in an illuminated Book of Hours
or kinship with Zen monks raking rocks
and meditating on *mono no aware.*

In the suburb of neat, small houses
sheltering under glorious Sacramento trees,
the leaf blowers fling the leaves back up again.
Swirled by the small cyclones,
showers of golden ginkgo, sycamore, ash,
settle down in restless mounds.

When I was young in New England,
our piles grew huge and fragrant.
We buried each other and hid deep inside.
Leaf fights presaged snowballs.
With a thrill of danger,
we leapt through twilight bonfires.

Leaf sparks rose and eddied toward the moon.
My hair smelling of autumn,
and dressed for bed, I gazed out
into still glowing embers.
Lying in the heat and ashes
were potatoes for our smoky breakfast.

Sixty years later, piles are taken up by city trucks.
Skritch-scratching fading green turf,
I contemplate the slower transformation
of red maples becoming compost.
Pause to pull impaled scarlet leaves
off bamboo tines.

EMERGENCE

I am invited to be the newest member
of the US Supreme Court.
I am proud to be talking to them on the phone,
and seem to hold a heavy cream-colored envelope
like a Nobel prize in my hand.
I am called. I accept.
A life-time position sounds wonderful.
I am surprised to be so decisive
and relieved about the future.
I firmly dust off my dream hands,
eager to get started on logistics.
Need to find a house surrounded
by trees in Washington D.C. ASAP.
Oh, and the physicians tell me I am pregnant.
I laugh and tell them
that is impossible, I am 64.

WEST

> *"But I reckon I got to light out for the territory ahead*
> *of the rest, because Aunt Sally she's going to adopt me*
> *and civilize me, and I can't stand it.*
> *I been there before."—Mark Twain*

It was a Tetris puzzle to fit all our stuff and camping gear
into our robins-egg-blue VW bug. Beloved books to be sent later.
A corner of honor was reserved
for our pea-green Hermes typewriter.
Peanut butter and homemade elderberry jelly sandwiches
spread on my whole-wheat bread were packed nearby.
My face wet after hugging my parents goodbye,
we were eager for the unknown adventure calling to us,
to travel across the country for graduate school in California.

Four years before we were married in our college's chapel.
Now, five carbon-papered copies of my husband's master's thesis
"The Archetypal Themes in Huckleberry Finn"
were now safely submitted to the University library.
My degrees in social work and management just completed.
His high school English teaching was finished.
We were leaving behind our families, still in small towns
in Massachusetts, Pennsylvania and Upstate New York.
They didn't understand why we wanted to move so far away.
To them it was reckless and they were afraid
they might never see us again.

First things first, I double-checked to find my birth control pills
safe in little bubble packs, rattling like seed pods.
Before cellphones, no GPS, just maps, signs, friendly people,

and our common sense—we found our way.
All behind us for now, forward we faced—West.

Tall graceful trees wound among the green hills of Missouri
along the Mississippi as we journeyed to Hannibal
where Samuel Clemens grew up.
We drove for days, talked, listened to the radio, read out loud,
and camped under cottonwoods in torrential rains.
We felt the flatness of the prairie, the red desert sands,
and saw thunderstorms coming miles away.
Our VW labored the inclines up over the Rocky Mountains.

In our sleeping bag, waiting for my husband to return
from ablutions in a campground with real restrooms,
I squealed when he crawled in the backpack tent.
Without telling me, he shaved off his beard of six years.
When we made love, it was deliciously illicit.

Through Barstow, we choose the scenic ocean views of Route 1.
Used to driving through three states in a day,
we couldn't possibly imagine how it could take so long.
No air-conditioning in the car, we sweltered.
Disoriented, tired, we were ready for a place never seen,
in a state where we had never been.

The surf and rocks below were wild, the winding road—scary.
The drought-parched hills of California were golden and brittle,
the smell of eucalyptus and jasmine—exotic.

16

Six months later, we stepped off our first ever airplane flight.
Back East for his only brother's unexpected funeral,
the air was wet-humid,
the land heavily lush with saturated green trees and grass.

Those first months in Palo Alto, I stood under the sprinklers and
imagined rain, adjusted the bathtub faucet to a slow drip,
homesick with the memory.
The hummingbirds at feeders I hung outside on the balcony
of our 11th floor graduate school apartment
were emerald, rufous, and red flashes—fighting and diving.
Every afternoon, fog crested like a slow tsunami
pouring in over the coast hills.
That whole apartment was smaller than our
San Francisco living room and kitchen.

In the fullness of time, heirloom furniture from both parents
trucked its way out West to our series of homes around the Bay.
Like so many others, we trekked to California and stayed.
Our born-here daughter went back to Boston, for a while,
to find snow and adventure.
Some people get the urge to go beyond the known horizon.
My desires are less geographical now,
but still risky and heart-pounding.

Easter Sunrise

On a dark hilltop, we shiver and stumble,
not quite awake, avoiding cow pats,
shoes wet with dew
Quiet nods to all around.

In pre-dawn the light grows.
With a first crack of sun,
a fumbled pitch pipe,
voices search for notes as we start.

For, lo, the winter is past, the rain is over and gone.
The flowers appear, on the earth.
The time of the singing of birds has come,
and the voice of the turtle is heard on the land.

Color suffuses the sky, rose light
touches our faces
and the wavering pond mist.
We call up the sun.

Hot chocolate steam rises in my face,
hands grateful for the warm cup.
I taste sharp, sweet citron, smell the yeast,
and lick my fingers, sticky with hot cross bun.

People smile, talk quietly.
When we see each other again in a few hours,
we will be dressed in new hats and egg-dye pastels.
Now, we are an intrepid few,
bonded with thousands of generations
as we sang night into dawn.

FORTY-SIXTH WEDDING ANNIVERSARY

I want to air-drop my dream
from my mind into yours.
You and I are kayaking
on blue-black satin-flashing water.

Dark mountains press glaciers
between peaks.
Pewter clouds are on slow roil
above our vulnerable heads.

Only our red eggshell kayak
is any protection from the immensity.

IDENTITY

My husband had a bad biking accident
during his last triathlon.
To avoid a collision with the speeding truck
of a hit-and-run driver,
he flipped over into the ditch,
inches from barbed wire.

When the nurse tried to remove
his remaining biking glove,
he asked to keep it on.

For five days in the white-sheeted bed,
the black, red and blue colors
of his incongruous gloved hand
caught all eyes
and reminded him who he was.

ABLUTIONS

Watching my father shave
in a white cloud of scratch-swath,
we talk. His attention is on task and me
and the rich lapping of the supple brush.
We talk about Mark Twain and Dumas.
I lay the badger bristles against my cheek,
wet fur springing apart, drying into softness.

Tap, tap, tap the razor on the porcelain sink
always three taps, then swish.
Like cleaning the sidewalk of snow,
the pattern is the same.
I regard his shoulders, firm jaw,
corded tendons in forearms
that taught me to hammer and weld.

Joining my tall husband in our warm bathroom
for his grooming meditation,
I daydream the son we never had—
his father teaching him razors and care,
eucalyptus and bay rum,
a green sharpness in the air—
a male mystery of steam and sweet soap.

LETTER TO MY SON

Dear Ford,

I know you didn't ever exist in real life.
I hope you don't hold it against me.
I am pretty sure you don't.
We thought about you a lot though—we did!

We fed the silky golden retriever you begged for,
held your hand on the sailboat tiller in blustery wind,
picked you up at the police station
for that reckless skateboard infraction.

Remember the tumor that almost killed you,
your shaved head from surgery in middle school?
Of course you do. I sometimes shake with relief
that it never really happened.

I see myself at your college graduation, so proud, I wept.
Your saturnine sister teased you,
flipped your tassel over.
Your Dad gave you his first edition of Emily Dickinson.

I miss you. You look like my father and your Dad's brother.
Our daughter never met either of them.
They died before she was born.
I smooth your dark hair, like theirs, out of blue eyes.

I am touched and thankful for your non-being.
Your Dad and I might not have stayed married
for forty-six years if we had two children.
The divorce, we didn't have,

did not scar your life. Some therapist, somewhere,
is tickled to not hear that story, one more time.
It is better this way, our wondering nestled in my arms.
I love you, my dear,

Mom

BIG THIS WAY

VALUABLES

A letter from my great-grandmother to my mother
reminds her that the pewter candlesticks, cameo brooch,
and tilt top table all came from
Great-great-great-grandmother Taylor.

She lived pre-Civil War, 170 years ago,
valuables in a straight line from ancestors' hands to mine.
The oak table is by my side of the bed.
I touch it each morning and evening
holding, as it does, bedside lamp,
lotion, alarm clock, tangled necklaces.
The surface includes an old burn mark,
and a new coconut oil ring, my recent addition.

In other parts of the world, 170 years is modest.
Here in my San Francisco house built in 1950,
surrounded by things we mostly hauled across country
in our blue VW, or acquired since, it feels long ago.
She couldn't vote, was chattel of my four-greats grandfather
and then her husband. Many children died young,
yet the women in my line kept a few gracious things.

Detritus vs. history, frugality vs hoarding,
I want to get rid of what weighs me down.
Some of what I keep now for sentiment or history
will have little resonance for my daughter.
I can not imagine the reality of her life
when she is my age.
I hope she values life more than any
of these things.

27

THE POWER TO CHOOSE

*"After the power to choose a man wants the power
to erase."—Stephen Dunn*

*Imagining my mother's loss of my three
siblings before they could be born.*

Blood ran down my leg,
again.

First the excitement, pride,
tempered with fear of something going wrong,
like before.
I held off telling the people at work
I was pregnant.

Pain, cramping, I saw the evidence
of our daughter,
my hopes, our plans,
in the toilet.

I didn't know
but I was sure, this time,
she was a daughter.
Despite the fear,
we named her Deidre,
in hope.
Sang to her,
willed her strength
to stay with us.

I chose to become pregnant,
again,
even knowing what might happen.
Erase my memory of her?
Never.

Not Until I Jiggle

Pink puff balls, soft meringues,
and sore nipples,
but my period hadn't started yet.
That happened at the Christmas Eve service—
blood on my latex girdle.

Between the nylons held with those clever clips
and the pressure of long leg spandex,
crescents of pink flesh blossomed like my breasts.
Thighs rubbed painfully, tight skirt
with a wide belt cut into my stomach.
Little heels hurt my feet.
Yet, I longed for a bra.
It was as if my status increased
with my quickly changing body.
But if I wore a bra,

I would become an instant public victim
of "turtle snapping."
The boys, almost all shorter than me,
would be sure to grab the elastic bra closure,
snap it back, and laugh.

My mother, her ample breasts poured
into an underwire she triple-hooked,
repeated her sartorial standard dispassionately;
Not until you jiggle, dear.

Settling An Old Score

Mom, you have been dead for 20 years.

I have tearfully raged at your ghost
for the gift of obligation I took to heart,
sacrificing my vitality—
first gladly, and then badly.

I channeled your coffee addiction and chain-smoking
into my over-work and dark chocolate
as we fueled control over ourselves and others.

Yet, I refill crystal vases
with sweet jasmine, verbena, and hellebore,
different from your forsythia and lilacs, a coast away.
Our sacramental prayer to the universe—
the same.

I accept you for what you gave me,
both dark and bright.
What I keep in my pocket now,
to remind me lovingly—
is my choice.

SECRETS AND DECISIONS

It is unacceptable and illegal for a social worker, physician,
nurse or clinic to break confidence
by telling tell parents that their daughter or son
has a sexually transmitted disease.

It is difficult to be certain
if a partner is using birth control,
except maybe a condom, which might break.

It is hard to tell by looking, at least for a while,
if someone is pregnant, and if they want to be.
Sometimes they don't know how they feel
until a pregnancy test is positive or negative, or later.

It is impossible to tell, by meeting them,
if someone had an abortion, or three, or two children.
Can't tell if they were relieved, or regretful, or both.

It is inaccurate to try to guess
how someone feels about their sexuality, gender, or body
without asking or having them tell.
They may not say, or want to say, or know.
It may well not be any of our business.

It is possible, indeed tempting, but ineffective
to tell a pregnant 14 year-old
she has no idea what being a mother will be like.
She needs all the help she can get.

It is unethical to tell
ICE or immigration police pretty much anything.

It is unrealistic to demand
that a purple-bruised woman leave her abusive partner.
It inconceivable to understand her full circumstances.
It is not our decision.

It is hard to be compassionate and non-judgmental.
But, we are not them.
Everybody deserves a hand up and a smile.

It is impossible to tell ourselves
we have done enough.

Infrastructure

It is such a strange thing to have my soul linked to my body.
For years, I suffered discomfort from cracking and crunching knees.
Then came hours and years of daily car commutes, hips
held immobile, right leg tense on the gas, and new issues with my back.
Not to be ignored, little foot bones misaligned in my ankles.
Gripping the steering wheel so hard led to arthritis in my left hand.

Becoming temporarily disabled and after, I needed a helping hand
up, now and then. I felt hot shame, sure everyone was staring at my body
from my graying hair, limping cane hobble, to my ankles.
Embarrassment familiar but this time I was so furious I wanted to knee
every one of them in the groin, and hope to see them flat on their backs.
Yet determined to ignore the pain and pity, I be so cool, be so hip.

The focus of my frame, center of pear-shaped gravity, are my hips,
always big, broad, eye-catching, and ample to hand.
Always there to remind me of childhood, thinking back and back
to taunts from schoolmates and Mother. My body
a locus of shame, diets and weigh-ins, tears bringing me to my knees,
too big and ugly all over, except 5' 2", eyes-of-blue, and trim ankles.

As I matured and grew into an improbable athlete, it was those ankles
that served me well, balancing me through triathlons, hips
swathed in biking shorts, so legs would not rub raw, thighs and knees
strong and powerful. I often came in last, earning cheers and a hand
from the race staff and dwindling crowds. Maybe they knew that my body's
effort and persistence were my pride, and I would be back.

34

I loved to run along soft paths in the woods, courses out and back
that let me stretch at the turn-around point and rest stressed ankles.
I was strong, big, happy, and more accepting of my body.
After years, sadly, inflexibility and pain started settling in those hips.
I went to the orthopedic sports doctor and she gave me a hand
with medication, and for a while, ache-free joints and knees!

I always imagined the infrastructure to go first would have been knees,
but it wasn't. Agony began radiating down one leg, was it sciatica, my back?
I got massages, hot and cold packs and rubbed my thigh with my hand.
I meditated, tried aroma therapy, and took to wearing an ankh ankle
bracelet to appease deities. X-rays finally revealed my osteoarthritic hips
must be replaced, bone sawed out, titanium added to my now bionic body.

Older, repaired and realistic, hips moving smoothly enough, back
to walking, knees no longer creaking, ankles firm, for now,
I caress my body and its tracks of scars, with loving and grateful hands.

GIRAFFE

A six foot five girl
is sheltering-in-place
in our house.
I am five foot two
and dropping.
I want to stare
at her tallness
as at a redwood.
I lean back
to see her.

In her life
ceilings are
reachable skies.
Spider webs
in upper corners
of patio doors
get in her hair.
Down the backstairs
she ducks to avoid
being foreheaded.

I am envious.
People see
my shortness
and plumpness.

She
rises up
a cliff,
a Rodin,
a Christmas tree
in Times Square,
bridge pylons
of the Golden Gate.

If I could have
I would have
chosen
to be big
this way.

THEY HELPED

I.
Early in my career as a chief executive
I felt beleaguered, beset.
I was never enough for my staff,
Board, donors, politicians, my mother.
After difficult days, I took stale bread
to the local duck pond.
The mallards flew and paddled
into a quacking scrum.
I was the center of their adoring attention.
The temporary respite buoyed me up.

II.
Years later marching in a PRIDE celebration
with the Planned Parenthood contingent,
I danced for a bit alongside a friend of a friend,
a young, shy man from the East Coast.
Normally formal and reserved, even distant,
he has felt the pain of being misunderstood,
more comfortable hiding his light.

Close to the front, helping hold our biggest banner,
he was blasted with the full-throated, roaring force
of acclaim, acceptance, warmth, respect,
and gratitude from thousands of people.

His face open, eyes bright, with a smile
that stayed for hours.
Each time I looked at him, walking strong,
he recharged my batteries as powerfully
as the cheers and claps of people along Market Street.
And a tiny plane in the bright cerulean sky
drew a giant fluffy heart.

CAR RACING THROUGH

after "Sleeping Faces"—Robert Bly

The steel cage and straps hold me tight,
my leg straining, cramped,
back quirked and pained.
Eyes squint, blinking
in syncopation with wipers
clearing the windshield clouded with rain
into the darkness of a two-lane highway
across the Bay wetlands.

Careening past random street lamps,
their watery beams only disrupt
my falling race through a black wormhole.
Oncoming cars only feet away.
Focus desperately
on the red tail of the car ahead
and faded white line. Ignore the dark water.
The car behind me is angry,

I am too slow.
Relentless rain stings the glass.
I am on the dropping edge between,
life and death,
hurtling past each machine,
trusting with mindless
faith they will stay in their lane.
I am only just a slight turn of a wheel,

just a phone call in dead of night,
just an unexpected diagnosis,
away from the ditch.
Drive blindly on, closer to home
and my husband and child—
faces in the dark.

CHAINS—WALNUT CREEK, 1980

Inside the health center, my co-worker and I
turn off the lights and kneel in darkness
at the picture window, trying not to be seen.

Outside, flickers of candles eddy,
and move in loose circles
like slow fireflies on a hot summer evening.
Chants, prayers and songs fill the air.
Many of these hymns have given me comfort.

It is almost like Christmas caroling in the snow,
when elderly neighbors peered from windows.
When I was young, I sang with joy,
and linked arms with friends for warmth.

Tonight, these singers hate me, and our services.
This night, I am filled with dread,
anxiety, anger,
and pride.

Tomorrow, in this medical center,
twelve women will each choose to end a life,
the life of an embryo growing in her body.
Life conceived in love or violence,
ignorance or bad luck—
in the back seats of cars,
lavender-sheeted marriage beds,
or on beer-soaked frat couches.

Each woman will let go of a fetal life,
her potential child,
one she cannot commit to love
honor and care for,
for the rest of her life.

I help to finish arranging new paperwork,
wrap instrument packs,
and settle fresh flowers in the waiting room.
In the morning, the first day of our new medical service,
women and their lovers,
husbands, best friends, aunts and mothers
will walk a gauntlet outside.

The people outside will no longer be singing.
They will be brandishing signs, shouting:
Don't kill your baby!   Hitler was not this bad!
Faces avid and filled with the same cortisol
running through the veins of their targeted prey.
The clients kept walking and more came each week.

Two months later, a young couple with no appointment
pretends to desperately need a pregnancy test.
With compassion for their urgency,
we welcome them behind our locked security.
At a prearranged signal, both ran
and flung open wide the exit doors.

Teams of invaders, clutching chains and locks,
rush inside, with military precision,
to take over the medical facility.
They assault our staff in attempts
to chain themselves to exam tables.

No woman was in surgery, this time.
No one significantly injured.
Thirty people were arrested.
At their trial, months later,
I gave my deposition about our program
and was cross-examined under oath.
Newspaper reporters interviewed me.

The invaders were found guilty of assault and trespass.
Some went to jail, for a while, including their leader.
He was a well-trained ex-marine from the Vietnam War.

When it was his turn at the trial
he spoke at length from the witness stand.
I thought I could hear the bondage of guilt cracking his voice
The babies must not be murdered.
The children must not be killed, he said

I think I understood. He vowed to save these babies,
this time—
not like those not so long ago.

Rush

Down the middle of the winding mountain edge road
             (my car on the inside of the curve,
                engine laboring up the hill)
the skateboard kid
was coming down fast,
                 fast,
                      faster.

He crouches deep, leans out,
wobbles, trails his gloved hand
to make the curve.
Not expecting me, almost hits the car.
He would have side-swiped—hard,
and inevitably rebounded,
surfing the air — up and over
the curl of a non-safety-railed cliff.

His three friends wave as they speed after.
Deliberate dance with death.
Theirs and maybe mine.
Clutching fear cascades through me
as I imagine slaloming that descent.

I Take the Subway to My Therapist

I park the car and walk down the hill to the Muni station.
The subway platform is below, down nine flights of stairs,
one hundred and seven steps.
Harsh lights reflect off crumbling iron concrete
wet with underground water.

The train is loud and fast.
Black walls rocket past,
so close I could touch them.

People keep to themselves.
Hunched women clutch shopping bags.
Strapping young tech guys with nice shoes
listen to their own music.

There are women of all colors,
their hair blue, pink, glossy black
and grey-white, a touch of purple.
Most dressed in ubiquitous black
and jeans of San Francisco.

At Market Street, I step out
into downtown air funky
with cannabis and other organics.

Curved oak railings, golden brass,
and white marble floors echo to her office.
Inside are high sashed windows,
hissing radiators—iron patterns almost hidden
beneath layers of paint.
The old building survived
the big quake, 1906. Still strong.

My intent is to let go of my position
with grace, goodwill and kindness.

Fifty minutes up, I descend back into the earth.
Reaching my home station, I take my time
climbing back out, up the nine flights of stairs.

Those of us of who eschew the elevator
for the stairs, are diverse and few.
I am the oldest I have seen,
certainly the slowest.
More time and less time.

Emerging into the tree-laden air
of the Forest Hill neighborhood,
my cheeks are damp with the clear evening.

The Book of Hours

High in trees tall as spires
I stand shivering on a tiny platform,
a kingfisher on a branch
over a rushing waterfall.

In the smell of pine and sweat,
I press backward.
I must risk the fall—leap and grab
with my whole body, my heart.

I stand motionless.
Pine needles prickle my skin.
I can't be safe without abandoning the tree.
Or, I must climb back down.

Leafing through the book of illuminated vellum,
I find the intricate drawing of this moment.
I turn the page of my trembling hesitation—
light catches golden in my flying hair.

ELEGY FOR A CHIEF EXECUTIVE OFFICER

The letter of resignation is on the desk.
Sparks escape only I can see.
Music by Two Steps from Hell,
and burning sage scents the air.

Who will I be when I am not a crusader,
not a good or evil fairy?
Who will I be when each late night call
doesn't conjure break-ins, fire-bombs, gunmen?

After 37 years as a Planned Parenthood CEO
I choose to become born again—
spelunker, gardener, weaver, writer,
wiser inhabitant of my new chapter.

Monsters still exist to be slain or tamed,
golden rings to be unmade, or explained.
I was a culture warrior.
I came home alive.

PULL OF THE EDGE

I Love You

I love you as certainly as you love my shortness.
It is true, forty-seven years together, some of my fears
are yours, your dysfunctional habits,
and their invaluable flip sides,
are now entwined in mine.
Do we look like each other?
Our daughter looks like both of us.

We walk well-worn paths,
unspoken guard rails
spanning the depth and distance
between our rocky walls.
Holding hands we step together
into rushing streams
together, for worse and better.

We climbed through unsteady scree
of our parents' deaths.
Slogged the mud
and danced under rainbows of parenting.
Reaching an overlook for a moment,
we share a bottle of cool water.

I love you as certainly as I forget punchlines
and laugh again at your bad puns.
It is true, this year is a good year,
all in all.

ANOTHER STONE ON A CAIRN

Waves slam steep cliffs
spraying the barnacled basalt
only to retreat again
in wheezing sighs.

I emerge from my spare hut
into dawn. Albatross silhouetted
against a pale robin's-egg sky
call, dive and glide.

There are no other humans
on the wind-scoured island,
yet multitudes of lives—
jostling, calling, fighting, dancing, mating.
I no longer smell nests, ripe fish,
and the white-streaked rocks because

I have been here for months.
Sea breezes shift, carrying sweetness
of lantana, palo santo, and green dampness
from the next island across the strait.

Finches peck around my rough bench
in the growing light.
One tastes my shoelace, unafraid.
I log the new bird's short beak and forked tail.

I'll work for an hour, identifying and counting,
leave off for breakfast and Bach,
and prepare to climb the circuit of my island,
check the equipment, take measurements,
add sand grains of data to knowledge.

RELEASED

I have always feared bridges.
The road's bright curves and crest seem to end
suspended in air.
Yet there is a pull of the edge that draws me
to quick peeks, between girders, of the far opaque waters.
I can't allow myself to imagine earthquakes or tsunamis
and how the spindly legs could buckle, fold,
to drop with me into the bone-cold water.

My commute frequently took me over the Bay Bridge.
One day, I emerged into the light of the second section,
the new bridge, its span held by soaring steel tendons,
grand piano strings vibrating in the wind.

A load of white cornstarch packing peanuts
had been released mid-bridge onto the black asphalt
to bounce and swirl, tap against windshields.
Passing cars tossed them again and again
into snowflake gusts and eddies.
I yearned to stop and trace their trajectories.
Not possible in the roaring traffic.

A few freed from the churning tumult of the road
fly—arcing out beyond the tower's summit.
Unbound from their crushing boxes,
heedless of the height,
they fluttered fearlessly toward the ocean.

OF A CERTAIN AGE

Love or lust? Teacher or artist?
Who am I, what's important?
When I was in high school and college
I kept a journal, wrote poems.
Everything was vivid, raw, and urgent
for me and my friends. Music lyrics and books
pierced my soul and our hearts.

Then we landed jobs, mortgages, furniture,
and less time to contemplate the cosmos.
When I had our daughter,
I was firing someone at work and so sleep-deprived
I brushed my teeth with Desitin, twice.
I still wrote, but only lists, business mail, tax returns.
Journals were history on the shelf.

My daughter grew up. I was ready to leave my career.
Friends and I started to bury parents.
Some in my circle got divorced, or had cancer or surgery, or both.
We begin to ruminate about the time left,
what's important, wrestle with regrets, prepare for the next.
Our feelings rise with memory and gratitude.
Poetry leaks out of our fingers.

ESTIVATION

I have a den.
It is filled with light,
except when it is foggy.
Books stacked around close
are read and unread.

New ones teleport silently
to my actual and digital door.
I live on sustenance of journals and poems,
written and unwritten.

My profession of four decades—
reproductive health, sexual justice.
Quite the hot topic, always a flash point—
now it is searing.

I didn't mean to get out of the heat,
but it went down that way—
after the election.

Wrapped up in my blue alpaca shawl,
mugs of tea, extra naps, I am hibernating,
even trying to use up my fat stores.

I am gestating
toward a personal rebirth
as outside my burrow
the wintered world rages.

I am quiet, by myself.
Not just in my bedroom like Emily,
but sharing a limited palette of colors
so new shapes emerge without distraction.

It is not so offensive to me anymore,
or embarrassing, to seem, to others, dead.
They can think of me, if at all, as retired.

MY DAUGHTER WRITES BETTER POETRY THAN I DO

Sorting old files of maps, restaurant suggestions, idea scribbles,
some of my daughter's poems leapt into my hands.
Each was in a different font as she loves the shapes of words.
One titled "Ravens," and another concerned the meaning of
      "Things" in our house.

I have written poems to the same birds as they flip their
      uncaring wings.
I bemoan, love and describe the same clutter, thirteen years later.
She was twelve then, images colorful, phrases liquid and lyrical.
Even today her prose and occasional poetry brings tears to
      my eyes.

I am pleased, proud and yet envious.
Maybe I best leave off my doomed writing efforts.
Still, I created her, at least partly.
She is my poem and thus I am vindicated.

Speckled Brown Study

I am lying in the tingling heat
of a morning window.
I bask like a brown trout
half in and half out of shade.

Time wavers in a heat haze.
I slide through streams
of friends' faces, spots of color,
conversations, a net of images.
Passing cars sound like white water.

I am startled awake
as a purple finch sings
from a quick railing perch
out the open window.

Rising up,
caught by the future,
I am pulled to the bank, flapping,
water beading on my golden skin.

WE REARRANGE ENTWINED BLANKETS

The oatmeal beige sofa
moved with us to five different homes.
Every year we pile it deeper
with more patchwork quilts,
crocheted blankets and alpaca shawls.
The newest fleece is cornflower blue
and embroidered with my husband's name.
Mine, is hand-loomed
with purple and gray wool.

He and I settle down with sighs,
books, and silver computers—
leave the dinner dishes for later.
We face each other,
our backs securely hugged
by the arms of the old sofa.
Above our heads
are paired moons of lamps.

Skin touches
as our socked feet slide past
rucked up pant legs.
Limbs entangle,
one leg on the outside,
the other leg,
a long pressure
between each thigh.

Turning a page,
I reach to caress his toes,
close and snug in padded running socks.
We have used the same brand for forty years.
I wear the grey socks,
his have blue heels.

He rises to pop golden popcorn
and stoops for a kiss. Returns soon
with a heaping wooden bowl.
The scent of hot oil, chili powder,
and lime fills our house.

NAPA WRITERS WORKSHOP—ST. HELENA

Great oaks hurl themselves into the sky,
jutting up from the valley floor.
They are dark against undulating hills
in a fading peach sunset.

Creaks, snaps, ticks of redwood
fill dusky air. The veranda cools
from the bright heat of this day.
Crickets keep time as it slides by.

The women I could have been
crowd behind me, a comet's tail.
Misty fates and options
of the woman I will become

await me with patience.
I hold a moment of this me
with tenderness. A new me
will arise in the chill morning dawn.

CONVALESCENCE

The gentle, halting
walk. A bit
more each day.
The time,
honey-slow,

I savor his
familiar profile
in the fading
afternoon
light.

In the Hospital Waiting Room

Family members fan themselves with magazines
in warm September weather,
read, nap, fiddle with cell phones,
or wait in silence, finding meditation
in unexpected places, or frozen
like rabbits, hoping not to catch
the eye of ill tidings.

My daughter and husband, each
going under with two-hour surgeries
within a week of each other.

So here I sit, again—
a different hospital admitting department,
same screened fluorescent lights,
green chairs with vinyl covers,
pleasant women behind counters
registering patients and answering questions.

My loved ones now have the numbered
wrist band ticket,
we are in the in-between place,
before the travel.

Then "Estes" is called and they leave,
taking my heart.
Practice for that final journey
when family is left alone,
outside the swinging doors,
not allowed to follow.
Our task behind, to handle all
the books, extra clothes, and cell phones
and wait—my heartbeat absent—
for the word from above.

GOOD SAMARITAN

It was well past midnight in misty rain.
The street was deserted—
only late Christmas party stragglers
like me.
I could see his bony, crooked back through his thin shirt,
lit only in the harsh light of the empty bus shelter.
Hatless, coatless he stared out toward the dark ocean,
past the piled trash in the turn-around.
He was all alone,
at end of the #6 bus line, after the last bus.
It was cold. He was old,
my age or a bit younger with a harder life.
He didn't even turn as my car hesitated, slowed,
I just drove on by.

I'll Have This Dance

My daughter at three, twirled to songs,
loved to jump and shake,
exuberance in her smiles.
But she stopped at ten,
self-conscious, awkward.

I used to dance in my teens—
became too body-shamed,
too fat, too embarrassed,
easier to sit it out.
Still, I tapped my foot.

We are both wiser now.
We dance—contra, swing, hard rock, line.
I cheerfully started the dancing at business parties,
shake that booty,
role-modeling comfort,
others joining me on the floor.

If I can do it, you can. I am in charge of me.
Other people's discomfort, comparing bodies—
I laughingly don't care anymore.
Not my problem.
I came to dance.

I Miss My Curls

I used to have abundant springy pubic hairs,
twining them thoughtfully
when on the phone or thinking,
(at home by myself of course, not at work).
Surely I am not telling a secret,
doesn't everybody do it?

I don't anymore,
not wanting to stress the limited strands.
Now the gentle comb-over of a balding man,
I am regressing to when I was twelve
when they were new and few.
Now I have few, but not new.

In the late 60's, skirts required,
my unshaven legs were a political act.
I absent-mindedly stroked
my leg fur when reading.
Mine is gone now. Happens when you get older.
I pet my grown daughter's virgin legs,
when she suffers my touch.

I miss the leg and generous
underarm fuzz of youth.
Even my long, wavy hairdo is now coiffed short.
The depletion, depilation of my V
is not tragically distressing.

I don't feel my womanhood stripped away—
gone with my periods and firm breasts.

I'm just nostalgic,
like I miss patting my childhood dog.
India was her name.

Cans of Baked Beans

A surprisingly heavy cardboard box
had my eight-year-old name on the address label.
I had won a contest.
Maybe I guessed the date of the first snow
or the number of jellybeans in a jar.
My prize was cans of food.

I took them carefully, a couple at a time
down to the spidery, damp cellar.
There my earnest father excavated dirt
late into the night, building cement walls.
I added my proud contribution
to our nascent family fallout shelter.

We practiced drills in school,
huddled under third grade desks
as emergency drill sirens screamed over our heads.
Taught to shield our eyes from the blinding light,
then the imploding glass of the first pressure wave.
At night, we dreamed of nuclear bombs.

Excited by the shelter, I would play
kitchen or scientist in the small musty crypt,
lining my precious cans up on the cement,
reshuffling them frequently
according to color, size, cuisine.

My parents never said why
the shelter was never finished,
at a loss how to explain
surviving nuclear war was moot.
So the tins and air masks stayed there.
Mice ate the labels.

EVERYBODY UNDER THIRTY KNEW

I guess you knew the memes.
Because everybody else
shared the photos, links, tests,
giggles and "Awww's!"

Farmers dancing in muddy oxen fields
even made my national newspaper feed.
Maybe it is helpful
to world solidarity in silliness,
like Obama's "Call Me Maybe."

But the otter meme is important to me.
I had never seen this before.
Did you know that sea otters
hold hands when sleeping?

They hold hands like stuffed animals
tangled in my daughter's bed,
lovers tasting sunsets over ocean,
me and my husband at night
fingers curled together,
rocking in waves of sleep.

Quantum Superposition

Spread out behind me, a fanning peacock train,
multi-chromatic them—who could have been me.
Feathery echoes of other women, one dead
in that rainy night car crash I witnessed,
one with three children, mother at 22,
two strutted round the world's eye,
sculptor, professor, therapist,
divorced, mated again.
Elusive choices over,
gaudy colors set,
they follow.
This
is
me
now.
Moments sift
alone in clear quiet
at the hourglass narrows.
As I ponder, seconds slide,
ahead pours my unseen futures—
old women I can become, ancient
alluvial fans, delta of silt and slow sand,
rich waters of wisdom with fewer options.
More past, than remains to come, the future slips.
Streams and rivulets dissolve in ocean's lapping waves.

SOME GOOD DEEDS FOLLOW YOU

I have suffered death threats, my house and neighborhood picketed and leafleted. "Do you know about your neighbor? She kills babies." Who would have thought, years later, to see protesters again and have them recognize me?

As Chief Executive Officer for Planned Parenthood of Northern California for thirty-seven years, it was my job to walk through protests on my way to work. I let the local police know where I lived and what I did, but decided not to use a bullet-proof vest. The cortisol-swoop close to my heart when the phone rang at night was not about my aging parents or college-bound daughter but memories of multiple fire bombs. The smell of burnt paper and melted plastic is still in my nostrils. But I stepped down two years ago, completed my multiple tours of duty, retired, moved on, to become a writer.

Tonight, I was just a donor, about to attend the annual Planned Parenthood gala at a lovely venue in North Beach. I would be with colleagues and friends I hadn't seen for a couple years. Awkwardly dressed in shimmering blue silk, low heels, and a black velvet shawl, I was playing dress up. My friends, husband and I tumbled out of the Lyft into the familiar, but unexpected, milling signs, shouting and bull horns of an anti-Planned Parenthood protest. Despite the noise outside, the event was very successful and brought out many new supporters I didn't know—a wonderful and healthy sign for the organization. For once, I was not a center of attention. Just a visitor.

It was after, as we stood on the curb waiting for our Uber, that the protesters pushed close, and called out my name. "Heather!" they yelled. I could see a couple of them had phones out, probably recording. The responses on the tip of my tongue almost escaped my lips. I had been in seclusion with my poetry, far away from the current of dangerous and terrible political and legal threats to people seeking birth control, abortion, and true health facts. "Heather!" they badgered again, shouting questions. I felt a wave of pride and nostalgia, excited, for the moment, that they had remembered me.

There is a Moment

MIST IN THE CITY

Delighted with all manner of words,
my father would savor them out loud,
teaching me his favorites.
Makimono or kakemono, he smiled,
first letter like mountain ranges—horizontal,
or like a tree with branches—tall,
that's how you know the scroll's shape.

A rare early morning mist flows
through the low valley below our neighborhood.
The mounds of Twin Peaks are exposed.
Tops of Monterey pines float on a white current,
or are revealed like bushes on snow-blown fields.
Houses, utility poles and streets are submerged,
human intervention invisible.

Fifty-five years later
the perfect Japanese word for the scene
drops melting into my mouth.

Afternoon Sleep

I am waiting for the sun.
For time to pass.
Waiting for my daughter to get better,
to pass beyond pneumonia coughing fits.
Waiting for light to return to her eyes.

She lies still on the sofa
barely shallow breathing,
her chest weighted
by the blue hot water bottle.

Motionless lidded eyes,
she is an effigy on the sandstone couch.
Shadows slide down her face,
familiar as my own.
When will she die? Someday.

The wind in Monterey cypress boughs
is the sighing of constant river rapids.
A black starling flock swirls away
against the ash-gray congestion of sky.

Struck By Lightning, or Not

Summer evening thunder and rainstorms,
my mother would let me and my brother
sleep on the squeaky porch chaise and canvas cot
under musty camp blankets.
She knew we weren't in any more, or less, danger
outside than inside.

I could hear the thunder coming closer,
count on my fingers the seconds
from flash to thunder—
an illusion of prediction.
The brilliant flash and crackle and hiss
of a close lightning strike,
only then bombarded by the cascade of loudness.

It was good practice early
for facing fear much later
as I watched my daughter
first drive the car away by herself,
or resigned from my beloved career,
or waited for the oncology report.

The rain poured down hard
on the porch roof and sidewalk.
Wind-blown drops were damp on my eyelids.
Even with the passing rumbles
of the imagined bowling games of the gods,
I would still fall asleep.

WE SPRINKLED MOM'S ASHES
IN GUSTS OFF CAPTAIN'S HILL

I am forever cleaning up—
lemon cranberry muffins, scone crumbs,
skin scales, threads of gray hair,
particles of aging sci-fi novels,
tissue lint, t-shirt fluff, shoe mud,
purple fleece nano-junk.
I am already hip-deep in the dust.

Garden breezes waft
multisided, infinitely intricate pollen
felt in sinuses, not seen.
Elaborate orreries of viruses,
miniature forests of fungus filaments,
biomes of bacteria mixed with cooking oil,
sighs, belches, and bus exhaust.

I move the dirt and smirch,
big, little, microscopic and atomic,
from the wrong places to other places,
into recycling bags to bins and trucked away.
Virus wiped with paper towel
settles innocently into compost.

A year after her death, Mom's ashes
arrived in a cardboard box labeled
Harvard Med School, Anatomy Dept.

Her jewelry, silver, furniture, clothes,
were long since divided and dispersed.

Only an aluminum numerical toe-tag left,
we offered the rest to the wind.

Last night, the moon rose huge and golden,
glimmering, deep in its ancient dust.

San Francisco, 14th Avenue

Back from coffee, electric car silent,
I always slow in the middle
of the one-way road looking over
Outer Sunset and the Pacific Ocean.

I search the far horizon
for jagged teeth of the Farallones.
A sailboat perches on teal blue water
where trawlers fish at night.

Cloudy mornings catch a current's silver edge,
sky ribbons of smoke gray, pewter, indigo.
White caps churn the sea,
the hush of wave-crash.

The expanse of ocean
is in perpetual conversation
with the mutable sky.

In unexpected urban quiet
I pause on the narrow overlook—
thirsty for salt air and freedom.

Pacific Coast

The wind is knitting up the fog
with needles of redwood trees.
Fluttering skeins flow softly
through the forests.

A dense softness nestles
in hills and valleys.
The twilight and growing darkness
smooths out the blanket.

Rustling cypress boughs
murmur and croon.
Through shifting clouds,
the nightlight barely shows.

Reading Ferlinghetti
While Getting a Mani-Pedi

I sit reading Ferlinghetti's San Francisco poetry
getting a mani-pedi, pre-pandemic.
My feet are in lemon-scented hot water,
fingers held by a San Franciscan woman.

I can't understand the Vietnamese of her
giggle-gossip with co-workers.
Customers rest in chair thrones reimagining
our lives and nails in vermillion or purple.

Do all people, as they get older, decry and bemoan
the passing of a culture and cast of characters
from their halcyon youth?
He writes San Francisco is become a theme park,

a corporate mono-culture,
turning its back
on blue-collar workers, poets, and real art.
Real people, real life. The way it was, then.

But I see the Polish Culture Hall in the Mission
full of young, eager, hardworking techies
and awkward twentysomethings taking introductory lessons
in West Coast Swing and Blues, earnest in their efforts.

I see gay bars specializing in country line dances,
hipster corner shops making pour-over coffee, cold-brew,
almond, soy or non-fat lattes, mine is black mint.
Dreamer cousins work the counter every morning.

Muni buses, Lyft drivers, and people who are homeless
roam the streets of this small city. Children laugh and cry.
Out-of-towners still move here for a freer, more vivid life.
The twenty or thirtysomethings and others still live in crowded
       apartments.

In another fifty years, will some new wave of immigrants
push out the old, cause the poets writing today
to reminisce nostalgically on the passing of tech start-ups,
charming, awkward nerds, the old days when unicorns were real

and resistance meant something?
The surf, now higher on the edge of continent,
will sparkle in the mid-day sun.
The fog will still roll in at 4 PM or before,

pouring down between the breasts
of Twin Peaks into the basin of Potrero and Bayview.
Residents will build calf muscles hiking up the hills.
Ravens and crows call and tumble in the currents.

My daughter will be seventy-five. She and her friends
will recall fondly, the way it used to be.

Before I Make Like an Egg and Beat It

I twist a few oranges off my tree for morning breakfast juice.
Kale and parsley harvest will go in a smoothie tomorrow.
Thyme goes in eggs. Rosemary on the new potatoes.
A lemon's zest sprinkled on shortbread cookies.
In season, blackberries go in claymore-cut oatmeal with
        maple syrup.
Unlikely I will ever boil sap down again in my life,
feel damp steam, hear the fizz-net of boiling sugar.
But I remember.

I have picked blueberries and strawberries for pie.
Taken figs, persimmons, apples and apricots off their trees.
Crushed, cooked, hung and drained grapes to make grape jelly.
Kept alive sourdough starter, fermented dandelion wine,
Pickled vegetables and watermelon rinds.
Selected salad greens, leaf by leaf, their milky juices on my fingers.
Brushed dirt off carrots and eaten them.
I remember.

Popped cherry tomatoes into my mouth, warm from the sun.
Been frightened by a huge zucchini hidden under broad leaves.
Stolen rhubarb from the neighbor's patch. Ditto raspberries.
Cracked black walnuts collected off the ground.
Chewed the ends of sassafras leaves and mint,
sucked nectar from honeysuckle blossoms.
Munched violets and nasturtiums.
I remember.

Dug for potatoes and clams, found quahogs with my toes.
Collected eggs warm from chickens.
Helped my dad kill the same chickens for stew.
Tore corn from stalks, smoked corn silk, or tried to.
Dried field corn and ground it into flour.
Baked corn bread, English muffins, pudding.
I remember.

Before I make like an egg and beat it,
I want to nurse kombucha scoby into being.
Master baking my own rosemary and matzo crackers.
Smell cocoa beans fermenting in the hot sun.
Toss a real salad of Miner's lettuce, not just taste a leaf.
Grind and leach acorns into acorn bread.
Bake and frost a green domed marzipan Princess Cake.
Stir pomegranate molasses into muhammara.
Try making a baked Alaska, one more time.
I want more memories.

THE LONG MARRIAGE

The corners of his mouth tug
in a secret way
when he is setting up a joke.

Gazing at me
in desire or pride,
his brown eyes and jaw soften.

Similar childhoods, though states away—
the scent and rustle of autumn leaves
scuffed on our way to school,

solid singable Protestant hymns,
how to pump the brakes on winter ice,
summer thunderstorms, ozone in the air.

We tasted the scent of our college library stacks
where we would run into each other—
accidentally, on purpose.

After picking and pressing wine-purple elderberries,
we know how the simmering jelly sheets off the spoon
when it is ready to be ladled into mismatched jars.

He heard my father tell the story of my petting a trout.
I loved his mother's soft, graceful, white hair,
his brother's laugh.

They are all long dead.
But, they are in our daughter, my husband's eyes,
and we find their handwriting in pages of our books.

We share memories never spoken about.
Yet, remembrance lays down a redwood ring,
to be counted on.

Yes, there is well-worn friction,
glacial grooves scraped deep
over forty-seven years of marriage.

And in just the past year
he started falling asleep with one hand
tangled in my graying curls.

I Bought One of Those Weighted Blankets to Help Me Sleep

Mountain tears slide down rock faces
of granite and moss, wear away dust,
thunder into ravines and cataracts.
Moisture seeps through scree and soil
to drip, drip-feeding mountain roots.

Stalactites wet with sky and ocean
weep into still pools.
Caverns echo in the quiet.
Blind fish search in the darkness.
Their dreams rise like mist.

Weight of the rock overhead—
a heavy blanket in the night.
In morning light,
my pillow is damp with stony tears.
We are all alone in death.

THERE IS A MOMENT

when my eyes flutter closed
over my poems or bird books,
the words rustling and gathering behind my eyes.
Am I asleep or in dappled spirit light?
Watercolor faces of past boyfriends flow by,
my toddler dancing at the farmers' market,
saints perched on cathedral facades,
speckled meadowlarks, beaks wide open,
caroling in golden fields.
Someone is calling my name.

"If There Is No Other Shore"

from On Prayer—Czeslaw Milosz

I am journeying the ocean
that might never end.
Leaving behind my
rock-bound certainty
for the shadowed depths
and press of sky and sun.

In motion and sluicing sea
I sail in currents
under star-stitched skies—
alone yet accompanied
by albatross and dolphin.

Where am I sailing?
Saltwater surges in my veins,
drips from my eyes.

Pas De Deux

Within minutes, the hummingbird tastes
the scrap of flowered cloth tied to the deck railing
and finds the sugar water.

By the end of an hour, it chitters loudly,
announcing the inclusion in its territory.
of this huge, crimson, nectar-rich flower.

I am in confinement, but not solitary.
The bird's twirling flight is free of
masks, taxes, poverty and politics.

Six feet away from where I sit
The hummingbird quickens my breathing.
We make our bright, tiny lives sweeter.

Margaret Mead and I

Settled in worn armchairs
of her cabin studio, we gaze out
broad windows of a slanted afternoon.
Out to the sky's beginning
stretches the flat expanse of wetland—
marsh grass, tules, and silver water.

Her hat hangs on a wooden peg,
the walking staff leans nearby.
Books, feathers, and Samoan art
clutter remaining walls.

Canada geese fly in formation,
touch down as we talk, settle into water,
shuffling wings, wagging tail feathers.
They join ruddy ducks with startling blue bills.
Mallards and buffleheads mingle
with a prayer of snow geese.

First time I visited, I was choosing
motherhood, or a different path,
envisioning the imprint of my feet on the earth.
Second visit, we contempated
my next chapter—
to sing ballads or defend again a fragile wall.

She questions and listens,
invites me to ask about her life.
Not a trained therapist,
she doesn't hesitate—no boundaries.
Just like I expected.

A wise older woman—not my dead mother,
or just a bit—curious, demanding,
a tough old goat.
We laugh.
Lapsang souchong steams in cups.
Starlings ripple in the darkening sky
like gray northern lights.

About the Author

Heather Saunders Estes grew up in a small New England town. She and her husband drove their blue VW bug to the Bay Area, sight unseen, 45 years ago. The blue jays looked different but crows, the same. Summer fog replaced winter snow. She lives in the Inner Sunset neighborhood of San Francisco with her professor-writer husband of 47 years and is sheltering-in-place with their biologist-writer daughter.

When Heather left her valued, long-term career as Chief Executive Officer of Planned Parenthood Northern California after 37 years, she transitioned to writing poetry. Poetry is laughter, reflection, appreciation, and a call to action. *Cloudbreak* is her second book of poetry. *Inner Sunset*, her debut book, was published in 2019 by Blue Light Press.

Her college academic training was in ceramics and elementary art education from a small college in Upstate New York. She had stints as an organic bread baker, secretary with 4-H, teacher in her family daycare home, and staff at a group home for emotionally disturbed girls. Subsequently, Heather earned a M.P.A. and M.S.W. from Syracuse University in health policy, administration, and direct services.

Always, ever since she became a patient, she has been a clinic volunteer, counselor, educator, donor, and Board Member or staff with Planned Parenthoods. She currently volunteers and advocates for LGBTQIA homeless youth services.

To schedule readings and book-signings or invite Heather Saunders Estes to speak at your book club, please contact her at her website or contact the Publisher.

Website: www.heathersaundersestes.com

CPSIA information can be obtained
at www.ICGtesting.com
Printed in the USA
FSHW012154050621
81984FS